LOVE AND ZEN IN
THE OUTER HEBRIDES

Love and Zen
in the
Outer Hebrides

Kevin MacNeil

CANONGATE

First published in Great Britain in 1998 by
Canongate Books Ltd
14 High Street Edinburgh EHI ITE

10 9 8 7 6 5 4 3 2 1

Copyright © Kevin MacNeil 1998

The publisher acknowledges subsidy from
the Scottish Arts Council towards
the publication of this voume

British Library Cataloguing-in-Publication Data
A catalogue record for this book is
available on request from the British Library

ISBN 0 86241 812 7

The seven poems by Paul Caudel are excerpted from
Cent phrases en éventail, copyright © Editions Gallimard,
1942, and are published in English in *100 Movements for
a Fan* (Quartet Books Limited, 1992). 'The Days Flash
Past' by Iain Crichton Smith first appeared in Gaelic in
Eadar Fealla-dha is Glaschu (Glasgow University, 1974).

Typeset by Antony Gray
Printed and bound by
Cromwell Press, Trowbridge, Wiltshire

Dhan reul-iùil agam,
a' deàrrsadh fhathast

To my guiding star,
shining on

ACKNOWLEDGEMENTS

Sincere thanks to the editors of the following,
where some of these poems first appeared:
*An Cànan, An Tarbh, Carmichael's Book, Chapman,
Edinburgh Review, Geum, Lines Review, New Ch'an Forum,
New Writing Scotland, Northwords, Spectrum,
Talus, West Coast Magazine.*

Special thanks also to Andrew Greig and
Aonghas 'Dubh' MacNeacail for striking a fine balance
between discipline and encouragement.

Many thanks to the Scottish Arts Council
for the Writer's Bursary.

Finally, wholehearted thanks to family and friends
for being who you are, and for giving me a
sense of who I'd like to be.

CONTENTS

ag ionnsachadh na h-ealain

learning the art

Your mind makes out the orange by seeing it, hearing it, touching it, smelling it, tasting it and thinking about it but without this mind, you call it, the orange would not be seen or heard or smelled or tasted, or even mentally noticed, it's actually, that orange, depending on your mind to exist! Don't you see that? By itself it's a no-thing, it's really mental, it's seen only of your mind. In other words it's empty and awake.

JACK KEROUAC (*Dharma Bums*)

Learning the Art

Well, when people ask me to teach them storytelling, I firstly teach them Burglary. As you know, my father was an expert burglar. In truth, he was so light-fingered he used his fingers instead of cutlery, even with soup. *Seadh,* when I saw him getting on a bit, I figured, 'He won't be robbing long, just who is it will be the breadwinner of the house unless it's myself? I must learn the art.'

I told my father and he was more than chuffed. So one night Dad took me to a house (I won't tell you whose) and we broke through the fence, entered the house and found a large kist. Dad says, 'In you go, son, never mind the risk. Just take out the clothes that's best.'

I went in, and didn't Dad drop the lid, lock me in, and run for it! He left the house by a window, and hammered on the front door. Everyone woke. Dad meanwhile went out the hole in the fence and of course the Mac – uh, the family involved – got up but saw no one. Well, shut up in that chest, I cursed my father stupid. I was mortified. And then an idea flashed in my head. So I makes a noise like rats gnawing. The old man of the house tells his son, 'See to that rat.'

Next thing, the lid's unlocked and raised and I snuff the guy's candle, push him away and break for it, six of a family in hot pursuit! Spotting a well by the road (and you would all know the one) I picked up a huge *ollag* and chucked it in. My pursuers gathered round, thought I'd fallen in.

Meanwhile, I got safely home and screamed blue murder at my father. Calmness itself, he poured a dram. 'Don't be like that, son, just tell your ole man how you got on.'

I told him then what I just told you. He whirled round, offered me a glass, and grinned: 'Here's to you, son. You have learned the art.'

seadh – well, anyway
ollag – large stone

Exile

The evening star hung motherpolished bright an inch off the moon's 1950s face. You raised liquid jewels all night in a Canadian bar, then sailed your foreign boat homewards through varying salt breezes.

Lewis floated towards you, smaller, perhaps, than anticipated. You poured an hour's silver tears on the Lewis Public floor, tore the wall off its hinges and ran to the pier where your people's bones first turned to salt.

You clasped two bloodied hands together like a single stiff spearhead and aimed it at the gloomering, pinned-up sky.

You wanted to pray but could remember neither the words themselves nor the accent which fixed them.

You leaped off the pier and, tossing your head back, made a mental note that you had never seen the stars shimmering so bright, so remarkably close. The sea drank you in, its splash tingling all over your body, as tantalising as a kiss.

Crush

He could not judge the state of her mind, not even a dozen years ago when he'd had a lingering High School crush on her.

He did not go to her wedding on principle – the principle being that she was marrying The Seaweed, a man whose face, as they say, could turn a funeral procession up a cul-de-sac.

Why, though, had she stopped speaking to him? Was she angry? And if so, why? If anyone deserved anger, it was him, because he – a bachelor – still loved her deeply whereas she had married The Seaweed.

When he saw her, usually on a Saturday in Roddie Smith's buying a *Guardian* and a glossy magazine – *Cosmo* was her favourite – or in Woolies leafing through the CDs (Cassandra Wilson, Buddy Holly, R.E.M.) he always reclaimed his gaze with a split-second laziness that embarrassed them both.

It frequently occurred to him how *complete* her life was – a cottage in Lochs, marriage, a wealthy father – in comparison with his sorry life (a council flat in Stornoway, a crumbling boat, a shrinking circle of friends). Why did High School hardmen like The Seaweed, who could barely write and had taken insane pleasure in smashing fire alarms towards the end of term – why did that sort prosper in life whereas he – who had been resolutely *dìcheallach* all his school-going days, found himself shaking, at times, with depression in a draughty grey council flat.

She meanwhile slept in the same bed as The Seaweed.

The Seaweed slept in the same bed as her.

He remembered her in music class. Her fingers assimilated new jazz chords like the dance of a wee girl's legs on wet stepping stones.

dìcheallach – diligent

One airy blue day in that classroom she had held his hand and had allowed him to kiss her and it seemed as though her love flew around him like a boundless net. After an initial shyness, he grew confident and told her a barrage of jokes.

He could no longer remember his jokes but he recalled how her laughter was pure and melodious as a diamond bell. Sitting on his cold bed at night he would hear this bell and resolve to ask her next Saturday why she no longer spoke to him, what he had done wrong.

The Storm

The old man listened to the storm, which said *Death*. He nodded. 'We'll go hack to the pub.' The younger men agreed with him and turned back, even Uilleam Mòr. Later that night, Uilleam's wife Seonaid scorched his back with small sighs as he waited for the warm touch of her breast. Anger sometimes isn't really *real*, they were both thinking.

Sleep came, and an argument between a fickle mind and a drunken, rolling boat. A moon made of skulls and bonedust sailed past singing the opposite of a lullaby. She woke between sweating sheets and noticed that her husband's eyes, which had previously been dull as bullet holes, were alive with inner movement and had adopted the colour of the sea.

Calum Dall's Story

Well – the *sgleog* on my nose? – yuss, thursh a story behuind that one ruight enough. It woss last Wetinstay – or Thurshtay reeulee – I woss ceilidhing late meekseeng drams an chokes with old Dòmhnall Beag. *Co-dhiù*, at last it woss time for the off, I knew, since the peats had grown coldur than our kwee-ur fish ministur. An chust as I woss out the door didint Dòmhnall call mee back an shuv a torch in my hand! 'You're drunk,' I said, 'giving the bluindust man on earth a tortsh to find his home! Day an night is chust the veree same to mee as yoo well know. I've trekked back an forth ovur that moour so menee times my feet have dug a trensh deepur than a peat bank!'

'*A charaid*,' he says, 'I know it's olwiss dark to yoo but thursh uthursh not so yoosd to it. An with Uilleam's grandson's dans on at the hall, yoo bettur take that tortsh so uthursh see yoo fursht an don't run into yoo.'

Well, I thot that woss good! 'It's yoo that's got foresight consitureeng you're half-shtewed! Well, *tha e fuar – tha mis' a' falbh.*'

I woss windeeng my yooshooil way across the moour. It's two miles it is an even if the moour woss as soft an springy as Iain Bàn's bread I woss makeeng good prokress. Blind or no blind, I'm as nimbil as the deer. An there woss mee sweengeeng Dòmhnall's big tortsh in frunt like a gun an still entshoyeeng the smell of whisky on my breath. BANG! Didint suhmwon run square into mee an I thot it woss the devil himself – chust as happind to Alasdair Mòr who called the

dall – blind
sgleog – hit, slap, bang
co-dhiù – anyway
a charaid – friend (vocative)
tha e fuar – tha mis' a' falbh – it's cold – I'm away

ministur's wife a two-faced – anyway who was it but Pàdraig MacLeòid whose fat head made this cabbitsh of my nose.

'In the name o the wee man,' I says, 'you must be bluindur than I am. Can yoo not see this tortsh, an it the brightest thing this side o the Butt o Lewis Lighthouse? Chust wotsh it in fyootshur!'

'Brother,' said Pàdraig, 'your batteries are dead.'

Hiort

The stars are spangling in the sea – the old glow, lust, an inter-mingling of downed vodkas and disco glances. What lacks in the spaces between the stars is the lacking of years; the sky is gloomering like a young mind still thirsting for soft words and travel and light.

His oars are angled and absurd, they are two wet tongues shaking in his dreamlike hands. He closes his eyes and pictures her in the green light of Chagall, a child painted faintly on her cheek like an ultrasound scan. Funny how he feels ugly when not in her presence. He rows on and on towards Hiort. His home is a vanishing bell. His child will be shiningly beautiful.

'The tree,' his grandfather used to say, 'shall be known by its fruit.'

The night before his physics exam, he had been feverish. The morning's cold light revealed a poem lying by his bed, in his own handwriting:

grandfather

> *history*
> *pinned on your breast*
>
> *in a way*
> *the stars really do hold up the sky*

He has never been out this far, where he has no permission to be. This is where his grandfather drowned.

Somewhere beneath this boat, *Seanair* burst and rotted.

Uilleam Sona's Song of Lewis

(To Murchadh Beag – and Lewis in general –
on the occasion of his departure)

Eyeland of brinebitten stone, eyeland stedee an grey, eyeland of
kristsheein nureeshment, to mee yoo are chust like some hyootsh
froe-sin saa-mon, quietlee wise in the Celteek way. Great preepacitsht
fish gifteed from God, yoo are as if sleepeeng, yea, eevin undur skies
as hevee as a neekname's eye-rinee: an I tshooteefoolee pletsh yoo my
undyeeng love, what with mee beeing premeeur bard of the villitsh.
Seadh, it is of yoo-ur bald an tighteyed men I must seeng, an of yoo-
ur heveewait *cailleachs,* speweeng fresh gossip into the constint salt
air. Loois, yoo solid grey windswept fish, this salt is God's way of
preserveeng yoo. Yoo are an Eden to us, yoo-ur tshoodishil gardinursh,
an I shall also seeng of yoo-ur sweengs an roundabouts, like
murdurursh, so rightlee strangild eetsh Saturday night: for it woss
not hilaritee whitsh got mee where I am today. That credit, of coursh,
goes to my Granee. But oh! sharpur than vineegur woss the time I
left yoo, *a ghràidh,* undur some preetenshis powursh: an oll yon
collitsh tot mee woss that thou hast thine own calidoneein anti-
sysitheeng, with thine urlee doe-ursh an yet purminint dreenkeeng.
O, eyeland of kworees an fish, Loois *a ghaoil,* my veree sustinins –
hapurr kareektursh yoo protshoos! They are a bettur medisin than
laftur or booze. It woss onlee today Murchadh Beag woss compelt by

sona – fortunate, blessed
seadh – well, anyway
cailleachs – old women
a ghràidh – term of affection
a ghaoil – term of affection
hapurr – such (emphatic)

the Lord to leev the place – Murchadh who, aftur won parteekyoolur sevin day bendur, woss transforimt by Grace. O, and cam untshayntsheeng tshurtshyard, gardin of stone, Eden of sensibil practeesis, though I have *not yet found the coorim,* I take my tablits safe in the nolitsh that yoo-ur fragrint an bounteefool presins, like ingraind vurshis of kristsheein text, like the print flavurd rapur that cradils the fish, will be within me and about me for all my dry days.

not yet found the coorim – not yet been converted, i.e. to the Free Church

Joy in the Hebrides

One day, they pushed the boat out. He rowed unspeakingly and in a few lengthening minutes they were a considerable distance from the shore. It was looking, as they say in Stornoway, very *mì-chàilear*. The sky was a marbled print, porridgy grey and watery blue. The great bulk of seawater slapped its unthinking rhythm on the creaking body of the boat. He pulled the sleeves of his *geansaidh* down over his clammy hands.

Her face opposite him shone with its usual lunar paleness. It occurred to him that she was scrutinising his own face as though searching for something new. He paused, then moved over to her. He leaned in close, observing that, like a Celtic manuscript, all her beauty was in the detail. The dolphinsmooth curves of her cheekbones, the dawnstained miniature pillows of her lips, the ovenbread mist of her flesh.

When their lips touched, they seemed to bring about a small electric charge. Her warm tongue slithered into his mouth, all strawberries and milk.

When he withdrew, when he opened his eyes, the light around them seemed to have strengthened, as though everything were reflected in highly polished silver.

At that moment, though, without warning, he felt a third presence nibbling like a squirrel at the edge of his joy. His father's boat was rounding the Rubha Glas like a gangster, like an ex-boyfriend.

He blinked suddenly, smacked the oars down and spun the boat round.

mì-chàilear – unpleasant, gloomy
geansaidh – jumper

Na Reultan

B' àbhaist dhomh farmad a ghabhail ris na reultan, an dòigh anns am biodh iad a' bruidhinn ri chèile, a' leigeil sradagan san t-sàmhchair dhorch, man bàird a' sgrìobhadh dàin mhòra ann an seann Ghàidhlig. Ach, oidhche a bha seo, bha na reultan a' bruidhinn ris a' Chuan Sgìth. Bha mi nam aonar 's cha b' urrainn dhomh dèanamh a-mach na bh' aca ri ràdh. Thuit rionnag gheal bho na speuran. Shnàmh mi a-mach sa mhuir fhuar ach cha d' fhuair mi idir i. An ath latha, dhùisg mi le ceann goirt, le aodann lainnireach ùr ri m thaobh, 's clach throm nam chridhe. Thàinig neul nam cheann nuair a dh' innis mo ghaol geal ùr dhomh gum bi rionnag aice nuair a tha a' ghaoth a' spiolladh mo chnàmhan.

The Stars

I used to envy the stars, the way they spoke together, sparking in the dark silence like poets composing mighty epics in ancient Gaelic. But, one night the stars were in conversation with the Minch. I was alone, I could not make out what they had to say. A white star fell from the sky. I swam out in the cold sea but I did not find it at all. The next day I woke up with a sore head, a shining new face beside me, and a heavy stone in my heart. I grew giddy as my new white love told me a star shall be hers when the wind is picking over my bones.

Fishing Boats and Ferries

She swayed past the fishing boat towards the ferry. She passed by the old seastairs and, after glancing to her left, turned and flashed a smile at me. A *taibhse* of wind shivered past.

A familiar incense glowed in my heart! Her eyes, her teeth, glittered like a sharp noon frost. Her lips were salmonpink, *gu math Leòdhasach.* Her smile had no charm, but a native confidence, something straightforward, like simple food delicately prepared. She seemed to exude a proud – no, a carefree – simplicity.

I frowned instinctively.

A deep stirring in me said, 'Call her! Pull her towards you!'

My reverie was jolted back, back under the mental horizon, by a loud, asthmatic coughing. Our engines spluttered into life, spun us slowly away from the quay. As our home floated past the ferry, she was leaning on the handrail laughing in the lilt of a greasyhaired student's mock-*Hearach* accent.

That night passing Cape Wrath, she appeared in the radar and in the finally opened letter (four years old it said, 'Like Wu Tsao, "You glow like a scented lamp in the strengthening dark. *A ghràidh,* let's buy a shining red boat and sail into the sunlight!" ') and in the fruit tea and in the tilley lamp, which survived the break-up intact.

taibkse – a ghost, apparition
gu math Leòdhasach – very Lewis-like
Hearach – Harris-like
a ghràidh – darling (vocative)

o ghrunnd na mara

from the ocean-floor

– and I wondered what the hell a butterfly
was doing out there at that time of year, especially
as it fluttered away seawards.

KENNETH WHITE
(*Travels in the Drifting Dawn*)

A Farewell Note

The one sound uglier than silence –
the skin of her palm
snivelling the bannister.
Good riddance hissed up, shadows clicked shut
the way a key is encouraged.
She left him perched high
to digest the meaning
of an over-rehearsed
phrase: 'Creative Healing'.

So; the curtains yawned,
a moon spewed gold.
The bare wart-bulb breathed
and glowed, heavy silence
cowered on the floor.
When he picked himself up
a new quiet composed
around his pulpit music stand.
She said his music could heal the gods.
The stand strafed with yesterday's socks.

Snow and Salt

Trudging Princes Street in an unexpected winter
heavy with Ishouldhaves and a Gaelic carrier bag,

I can no more shake you off than
convert the Wall of China into a rollercoaster.

(How noble it is to be a man and thus have influence
over love or weather just as a flea adds

to the gravity of earth and hence the stability of Jupiter.)
Can we bring about a change in love? I believed once

that snow was a chill test, silent, bearable,
like the air in a ship which exiles share.

Yet, in this snowstorm, unending and timeless
as white jazz, as thoughts of a girl filled my eyes

with tears, snowcrystals settled on each of my irises.
Improbable, snow, I should love you! Like a comet, you
        bring us relevance.

I picture you drifting through aeons of starry flakes
passing on (unnoticed, say, as one-sided love is),

later to surface, purer, water that is more
than water, a snow-white comet launched in the night

of our grandfathers' grandfathers, whose purpose drops it
with a blinding fizzle into the brine

of a shining green sea-loch, as though to absorb
the first taste of salt could set in motion

a sea change, an ice age, a thirsting for dilution.

Balbh

Bha mi ag iarraidh dàin is todaidhean
is sìth-inntean a thoirt dhut.
Chunna mi thu an-diugh
's cha robh càil ri ràdh
ach anns a' bhad fhuair mi a-mach
cò ris a tha e coltach
gach uair a chì thu mapa
's chan fhaic d' inntinn càil
ach seo far an d'fhuair iad a bhàta.
Chan fhaic mise càil ach mi
fhìn a' snàmh gu mall
tro rùmannan uaine d' inntinn,
mo ghàirdeanan a' faireachdainn
nan tonn troma man sruth
de ghlacan briste.
Latha a bha seo, chum thu deagh
ghrèim air mo làimh man failm
neo-mhuinighineach.

Dumb

I wanted to bring you poems and toddies and peace of mind. I saw you today and there was nothing at all to say but I learned in an instant what it is like every time you see a map and your mind sees nothing but this is where they found his boat. I see myself swimming slowly through the green rooms of your mind, my arms feeling the heavy waves like a stream of broken embraces.

You who once gripped my hand like an unreliable rudder.

Fiach

Ged a tha iomadh bliadhna air a dhol seachad
bhon thaisdeal naoi mìosan agam nad bhroinn,
tha am fiach agam ort fhathast cho farsuing ris an fhàire,
thusa a bhitheas a' cur eagal orm le dragh is ròpan is gaol.

Ràinig na tuinn thu, dh'fhàisg iad thu, chum iad thu, lìon
   iad thu,
mus do leum an stoirm suas mar uilebheist bhon àird-deas.
Lìon na tuinn thu le pian, tonn an dèidh tuinn làn
le sàl do-fhaicsinneach, mol maolaich, gainmheach gharbh,
   dòmblas dèisinneach

'S cha chreid mi ach gur e mi-fhìn a chuir snàim air an
   ròpa.
Dh'fhan thusa cho trom ris an fhìrinn air an tràigh,
a' laighe sìos nad' throm-lighe shàmhach fhèin,
's an làn-mara ag èirich mu do chuairt, searbh, fuar,
   neo-thruacanta.

Ged a tha mi a' feitheamh nise cogaiseach, iomallach,
   neo-chomasach.
chanainns' le cinnt gum bi thu ceart gu leòr.
Sàbhalaidh an dìoghaltas neònach seo thu, chì thu
   làithean ùra,
is bidh thu beò (tha mi 'n dòchas) fhad 's a bhitheas
   seòladair na h-inntinn seo beò.

Debt

Though many years have passed since my nine-month voyage in you, my debt to you is still as wide as the horizon, you who scare me with worry, ropes, love. The waves reached you, they pinched you, they kept you, they filled you, before the storm sprang up like a beast from the south. The waves filled you with pain, wave after wave filled with invisible brine, blunt shingle, rough sand, nauseous bile.

I believe nothing but that it was myself who put a knot in the rope. You waited as heavy as the truth on the shore, lying down in your own silent nightmare, the tide rising about you, bitter, cold, relentless.

Though I am waiting now remorseful, remote, impotent, I would say with certainty that you will be all right. This weird punishment will save you, you will see new days, and you will be alive (I hope) as long as this sailor of the mind is alive.

pòg

pòg
fàileadh lag na mara

a kiss

a kiss
faint smell of ocean

Flying Geese

I've read that poem, the one about the geese
flurrying past utterly mindless
of their being reflected

and I've reflected on the lochans
'which have no mind
to receive their image'.

At the rickety brown desk to watch the evening
geese arrowing past, clamorous
and lofty as the ambitions I harbour:

only to craft poems, only to picture her
overlooking her admired image.

an acarsaid

na rionnagan a' deàrrsadh 'san uisge
na rionnagan a' deàrrsadh na mo chridhe
an Cuan Sgìth mar sgàthan dorch
's do phòg mu dheireadh
air mo ghruaidh fhathast
balbh, fuar, fad air falbh
mar seann ghealach
a' cuimhneachadh air acarsaid eile

the harbour

the stars shining in the water the stars shining in my heart the Minch
like a dark mirror and your farewell kiss still on my cheek – dumb,
cold, distant – like an old moon remembering another harbour

i should have kissed you

i should have kissed you,
not whispered as
the sea does when I walk
head bowed, through the cold foam

A.M.

'Dè mun a tha thu?'
Wet, your hair gleams. Heather dew.
Gems. Dharmadhatu.

Spring

Spring does not belong to the ordinary
senses. Watch how shadows deepen
and revive in the swooning sun.
(Their black glow is the quease and seethe
of jealousies I have known.)

Flowers settle, bees bubble with life,
miniatures of colourful lust.
(So, too, the dawn I arose by
my impossible love's side.)

Winter's bone-and-ice trees breathe light.
(They are buddhists rooted
in the warm flesh of fact.)

And how this universe, the dharma wheel, turns
to a woman's most intimate gesture!

(And how afterwards summer appeared
to astound us with its ordinariness.)

dè mun a tha thu? – how are you?
dharmadhatu – the universe as perceived in enlightenment, often imaged as a
myriad of sparkling jewels

The River Creed

Listen, is the course of words
a river in full thirst? My love,
this river runs absorbing salt
raised on the wind of repeated Minches.
The same salt wind whose breath
teases your hair, your blouses, your dresses,
enters you, binds us, and hence
this overwhelming thirst, this incessant river
bursting over and under and through
a reflected moon, which is you –
a pale face stunned,

               serene,

                  untouched?

The Creed is a river in Stornoway

Alone and Drinking

Sometimes I'm alone and drinking with you
as though you were here.
You hear the lessening bottle clink,
hear the splash to the brim,
that loved sound ebbing on each stiff pour?

The room grows dim as the ocean floor
as the bottle trips its last and perhaps
keels over. Already your ghost
which streamed like some ghoul-fish
round the vessel of my head
is gone. The bottle lies empty:
not drink would I wish into it
but a miniature sea-faring ship,
its fanned-out banners
bursting as it dips
to skirt the briny waves,
to breast the lapping wind,
its dry surging ruinous lips.

for the seabereaved

(on the isle of skye you are never more than five miles from the sea)

the waves are not preening themselves the waves are not preening themselves
the waves are not preening themselves the waves are not preening themselves
the waves are not preening themselves the waves are not preening themselves
the waves are not preening themselves the waves are not preening themselves
the waves are not preening themselves the waves are not preening themselves
the waves are not preening themselves the waves are not preening themselves
the waves are not preening themselves the waves are not preening themselves
the waves are not preening themselves the waves are not preening themselves
the waves are not preening themselves the waves are not preening themselves
the waves are not preening themselves the waves are not preening themselves
the waves are not preening themselves the waves are not preening themselves
the waves are not preening themselves the waves are not preening themselves
the waves are not preening themselves the waves are not preening themselves
the waves are not preening themselves the waves are not preening themselves
the waves are not preening themselves the waves are not preening themselves
the waves are not preening themselves the waves are not preening themselves
the waves are not preening themselves the waves are not preening themselves
the waves are not preening themselves the waves are not preening themselves
the waves are not preening themselves the waves are not preening themselves
the waves are not preening themselves the waves are not preening themselves
the waves are not preening themselves the waves are not preening themselves
the waves are not preening themselves the waves are not preening themselves
the waves are not preening themselves the waves are not preening themselves
the waves are not preening themselves the waves are not preening themselves
the waves are not preening themselves the waves are not preening themselves
the waves are not preening themselves the waves are not preening themselves
the waves are not preening themselves the waves are not preening themselves
the waves are not preening themselves the waves are not preening themselves

faclan, eich-mhara

nam bhruadar bha mi nam ghrunnd na mara
agus thu fhèin nad chuan trom
a' leigeil do chudruim orm
agus d' fhaclan gaoil socair nam chluasan
an dràsda 's a-rithist
òrach grinn ainneamh
man eich-mhara, man notaichean-maise
sacsafonaichean beaga fleòdradh

words, seahorses

i dreamt i was the seafloor and you were the weight of ocean pressing down on me, your quiet words of love in my ears now and again, golden, elegant and strange, like seahorses, like grace-notes, tiny floating saxophones

song sung dry

at night a frog trembling
on the edge of a well

even so the shiver in my chest
as I measure the voyage to Lewis

I should have taken the Minch
in a single leap if only to prove

how badly, how deeply I have fallen for you

i see you rising

'Dh' iarr am muir a thadhal.'
'The sea requested its visit.'

i see you rising over Lochs
and where your father sleeps
is pouring through your eyes,
his green boat, broken, cradled in your arms

the Minch is calmer tonight,
the waves uneasy
under a starry, disquieting, satisfying breeze

like an unshakeable

like an unshakeable sickness i feel you
are preparing us
for your death

i read your eyes
even as a
fisherman reads the sea

o ghrunnd na mara / from the oceanfloor

acras ga shlacadh fhèin
air an dubhan

acras ga shlacadh fhèin
air an acair

*

hunger thrashing
on the fish-hook

hunger thrashing
on the anchor

*

ràmh
peann mòr briste
a chuidich iad a' dèanamh
iorraim, a bha dannsadh
uair-eiginn
ann am bàrdachd fheumail

*

oar
a huge broken pen
which helped them compose
rowing songs, which once
danced
in a useful poetry

*

's math dh' fhaodte g' eil do chnàmhan
faisg air alba nuadh
's math dh' fhaodte gu bheil pìos dhìot
ann an iasg air
nach cuala mi riamh

*

it's possible your bones lie
near nova scotia
it's possible a piece of you
is in a fish
i've never heard of

*

latha breagha air
choir-eiginn, ithidh am muir
mi. cuidhlidh sinn fad
grunnd na mara
man dà smuain
dìochuimhnichte

*

one day the sea will
swallow me. we shall
bump along the sea floor
like two forgotten thoughts

All the clouds

And it would be simpler to contain all the clouds
in a single jar unlidded
than expect this love to be returned.
Just as the wind – breathless – carries a song
and never quietens its bustle to listen,
just as a bird's shadow streams over a lake,
just as our country exists and it doesn't,
and just as our world's original dawn
will never again equal itself, but rises blushing
that it be admired as a constant failing,
so you are here and are not here,
your face a bright mist in my dreams gently fading.

eadartheangachadh

translations

The poet moves from life to language, the translator moves from language to life; both, like the immigrant, try to identify the invisible, what's between the lines, the mysterious implications.

ANNE MICHAELS (*Fugitive Pieces*)

An dèidh Paul Claudel / After Paul Claudel

(1)

oidhche
air broilleach na
h-oidhche
fear dall a tha ag
iarraidh a bhith
na chadal

night
on the breast of
night
a blind man
who wishes for
sleep

(2)

Tha a' mhathair bheag
le ceumannan
luath
a' togail na h-iteileig bhon talamh
ach 's e am pàisde air a cùlaibh
le bheul fosgailte
a tha ga cumail 'san adhar.

The little mother
with rapid steps
raises the kite from the ground
but it's the infant behind her
with his mouth open
who keeps it in the air.

(3)

an t-seann bhàrd
a' faireachdainn sreath
a' tighinn air
mean air mhean
mar sreathart

the old poet
feels a line
coming on him
little by little
like a sneeze

(4)

Suidhichidh a' chuthag
an t-àite far
nach eil
sinn.

The cuckoo fixes the place
where we are
not.

(5)

beachd ri
taobh beachda

gruaidh ri
taobh gruaidhe

opinion be
side opinion

cheek be
side cheek

(6)

Isd!
(dèan fuaim idir
agus tòisichidh
tìm a-rithist)

Hush!
(make a sound at all
and time will start
again)

(7)

Ag èisdeachd

tha cuideigin
a' bruidhinn rium
le shùilean
dùinte

Listening

someone is
speaking to me
with eyes
closed

An dèidh Basho / After Basho

(1)

Bodach bochd – a' fàgail a bhith
coimhead air a' ghealaich
airson eaglais dhoilleir.

Poor old man – leaves
gazing at the moon for
a gloomy church.

(2)

Dùisg, a dhealain-dhè – tha e
anmoch 's tha mìltean againn
ri siubhal còmhla.

Rise and shine, butterfly!
It's late and we've got miles
to travel together.

(3)

Eun tìme –
ann an Ceòs
làn cianalas airson Ceòs.

Bird of time –
in Keose full
of homesickness for Keose.

(4)

Sgarbh ag iasgach:
cho brosnachail,
cho brònach.

Cormorant fishing,
how moving,
how saddening.

(5)

Am Foghar – fiù 's
na h-eòin is na sgòthan
a' coimhead aosda.

Autumn time – even
the birds and clouds
seem aged.

(6)

Càirdean air sgàradh
gu bràth – geòidh
caillt' anns na sgòthan.

Friends separated
for ever – geese
lost in the clouds.

(7)

Cùirneagan – abair
thusa dòigh rnhìorbhaileach
stùr an t-saoghail seo a nighe!

Dewdrops – what
an amazing way
to cleanse the dust of this world!

Tha na làithean a' dol seachad / The days flash past

(from the original Gaelic by Iain Crichton Smith)

The days flash past us
as we age.
What happened to the ballerina
in the mirror, what happened
to her unblemished face?
The twittering birds diminish
under the shaver's surly buzz,
the towel behind the door
becomes an apparition.

Ah, world, did you indeed deceive us,
or was it us who misread you
all those days your face was lying
open, reflecting back on us?

duilleagan sàmhach

quiet leaves

The wind brings
Enough fallen leaves
To make a fire.

RYOKAN
(One Robe, One Bowl)

beannachd

beannachd na grèine, beannachd an uisge
solus na làn-ghealaich air achadh reòta

blessing

the blessing of the sun, the blessing of the water
light of the full moon on a frosty field

Domestic

you came on her like the sun
converting the sea's agitation
into a living sparkle

your kisses blew away her griefs
the way a gunshot
tears birds from the trees

*

tingling jewels wrist deep
in scroggy brown dishwater

bird after bird returning
in smiles which flicker like a broken wing

Cremations Premature and Gradual

'So cremate me,' – she exhales –
'And have me buried in an ash-tray!'
It is a shining day and cloudless
but for her smoke. As though reading
his thoughts, the sun breaks
through the window, ravishing the plants
and his book. Satisfied, he finishes Dante
instead of the argument. She closes it:
'The Love which cancers earth and the other
planets.' Her fist is almighty.
She crunches the dead packet.

The Bar-Flea

Put a noose on that singer, pour me another
dram – have one yourself – and understand:
it is not the lily-fringed lochans of Lewis,
no nor the brownish black hills of Harris
I consider home.
Rather, it's in those wee small hours
and gestures – that special tin,
that crystal tumbler
overgenerously-f–i–l–l–ed
with whisky – aged, poor,
indifferent! –
when my black mood swings
to green affection
which seems to last until
I lurch back
into the chilling English exile
of Edinburgh: the grey kay-lees
in pubs like this, the smiles thinner
than tourist lies, the austere
gothic homes
brooding like gravestones
so that wherever I go
I am in W. S. Graham's
colossal poem
'like a flea crouched
in the stopped
works of a watch'
– which is really what yon guy
ought to be warbling about

and – what's that? –
you're going to throw him out
if I'll recite MY exile song?
I could, but my throat hurts
and my tongue's dry as rope.
Let's sit and do nothing for one more round.

Young Chinese and Scottish

These bastards I feed.
I serve them sourfaced
from this lair's fiery kitchen,
dish up oodles of rich-crispy-chicken
in an atmosphere thick
with soy, sweat and steam.

Ape-drunk, certain, they'll swagger in,
pie-eyed and slobbering on my thin
silken blouse: '(Hur hur) Hello rare
mah wee China doll, er . . .
Ah'll havvuh speshl (hur hur) sixty-nine
(hur hur) uhna bedduh speshl flied lice.'

My folks tell tales of dragons, but I have tasted haggis!
See, Buddha-sure, I just hunger for dancing, drinks
and a Scot I adore. How I love to not
taste homesweethome in his plain Scottish food.
I'll serve no more. Take away
the Chinese til I'm half understood.

quiet leaves

quiet leaves
floating against the snow
but slowly

each
one becomes
a hug you denied

in thickening mist

in thickening mist
a foreign joke sails between
the hills and this boat

a red flower

a red flower
bows behind the tree,
flush of a lost girl's cheek

in the graveyard

in the graveyard a
minister playing frisbee
with his elder son

Cnoc na Tùrsa, Calanais /
Hill of Mourning, Callanish

that I could be
as a tongue of sunlight
drawing slowly over Harris

Lewis Rain

The lash of a harsh
Lewis rain. Endless moor
and God's loneliness.

one of ours?

in the fairy loch
a satellite (faint)
winking

when i climb the cuilin

there is no wind, i climb at underwater
speed and there is only the pinprick
light of sluggish, longdead stars,
twinklings of her eyes, her ear
– rings in black gravity, a glistening oilslick

the violent blush

which burns on the sky
as he slips tinily away
into a returning distance
his faint white socks
tumbling after each other like sobs

Am Bogha-frois Briste / The Broken Rainbow

(1)

Cha tèid falamhachd an adhair na chriomagan
gu bràth. Thèid falamhachd an adhair
na chriomagan air latha fada dòrainneach
air choireigin mar phìos ciùil jazz mar
bhogha-frois a' briseadh an àirde.

The emptiness of the sky shall never crumble. The emptiness of the sky shall crumble some dull day or other like a snippet of jazz, like a rainbow disintegrating.

(2)

Nuair a bha mi òg
bha mi man tìgeir ach
tha mi nise man cat.
Am faca tu, a laochain,
deilbh Phicasso? Bhiodh e
a' peantadh man Raphael
aig ochd bliadhna dh' aois.
'S co-dhiù, dh' fhàs e ainmeil
a' feuchainn ri dealbhan
a dhèanamh mar ghille òg
beag imcheisteach.

When I was young I was like a tiger but now I am like a cat. Have you seen, my wee hero, paintings by Picasso? He painted like Raphael at eight years of age. Anyway, he grew famous trying to paint like a puzzled infant.

(3)

A' ghealach os cionn Steòrnabhaigh, ars' na bàird –
mòran nas fhaisg, mòran nas soilleire,
mòran nas cruinne, mòran nas fheàrr.
Seinnidh sinn sin, ma tha. Ma 's fhìor.

The moon above Stornoway, say the bards – much nearer, much
brighter, much rounder, much better.
   We'll sing that, then.
   (Aye right.)

(4)

Abair thusa sradag dhathail
man pìos bogha-frois gun
chudthrom idir.
Chan eil càil ann a bhith
nad dhealan-dè.

Such a colourful spark, like a piece of rainbow without any weight.
It's nothing at all to be a butterfly.

(5)

Mo nàbaidh. 'S e tòraidh a th' ann.
Tha stiocair air a chàr: Free Tibet Now.
Cha chaomh leis na prògraman Gàidhlig.
Money for a dead language. They all
speak English anyhow. Tha chuibhle mhòr
a' tionndadh na bhroinn
man spaid shlaodach bhiorach
anns an ùir. Tha rudeigin a' fàs an-sin,
cruaidh, man loidhnichean air aodann
cosnaich, cinnteach, man boma dearg
a' diogadaich ann am manachainn Tibetanach
ann am meadhan a chadail,
agus iom-tharraing do-thuigsinn
a' dol na chriomagan gu slaodadh eadarra.

My neighbour. He's a tory. There's a sticker on his car: Free Tibet
Now. He doesn't like the Gaelic programmes. Money for a dead
language. They all speak English anyhow. The great wheel turns in
his breast as a spade in the dirt. Something grows there, hard, like
the lines on a peasant's face, certain, like a red bomb ticking in a
Tibetan monastery in the middle of his sleep, an inscrutable gravity
crumbling slowly between them.

For the Curtain Twitchers

chust reemembur the dumb old man
one brethless, gossipeeng day
who leend against a window
an steemd it up so mutsh
he beleevd the window emtee,
the whole eyeland grey

Lost Loch Floating

Lost loch floating
behind the mist
summer
is over.

do dh' alastair macgillemhìcheil / to alexander carmichael

uaireannan nuair a tha mi
gam bhlàthachadh
ri taobh an teine-èigin

ann am bothan beag m' inntinn
chì mi d' fhaileas
air a' bhalla

sometimes when i'm
warming myself
at the need-fire

in the little bothy
of my mind, i glimpse
your shadow on the wall

Summer in Lewis
(after Buson)

on the tshurtsh bell
purtshd sleepeeng
a butturfly

painting trees

that every brush stroke
should, like fruit,
have purpose and happen

drum drumming

drum drumming your fingers
on the steering wheel
rain on the skerry

beady eyes

it's not that i cried but
my eyes sweated in the complexity of you

and a God still pouring stoically
over prima donna flowers

mirror eyes of dew

Gallows Hill, Stornoway

it's not that you don't bless us, Lord,
with blossoms in the shadow
or coppery *clàrsachs* of forest
etcetera but

our island stands there,
an abandoned card-table

blind dread

little snowy leaves
gazing from the tree

(cold appointment)

duff corneas floating
on the autumn breeze

from the other side of The County, her sigh

the seagull's feather
which burnt a plane's engines

Na Flùran

Thuirt mi ris na flùran: 'Tha sibh a' deàrrsadh.'
Dh' iarr na flùran orm: 'Cum ort a' leigeil d' anail.'
Thuirt mi ris na frasan: 'Is sibhse mo dheòir.'
Dh' innis na frasan dhomh: 'Seadh, 's sinne do dheòir.'

Is bha na flùran cus na bu shoilleire
cus na bu bheòthaile
cus na bu dhaonnaiche.

Eadar deòir
dh' iarr mi is
dh' iarr mi air na flùran:
'Cumaibh a' tarraing ur n-anail.'

The Flowers

I said to the flowers: 'You're shining.'
The flowers asked me: 'Keep breathing out.'
I said to the rain showers: 'You are my tears.'
The rain showers told me: 'As you say, we are your tears.'

And the flowers were so much brighter
so much more alive
so much more human.

Between tears
I begged and
begged of the flowers:
'Keep on breathing in.'

When your friends were fantasising

When your friends were fantasising
over Captain Kirk and Neil Armstrong

you lay between stormtossed sheets
projecting mental light

– houses into the restless Minch
where your father's accelerating rums

saw clouds tremble and shift
like a widow's dress like a child's

bunched-up grief, and glimpsed
stars – intermittently – candleweak.

East Over West

A friend of a friend, see, Japanese Scot
-ophile, richer even in mind
than wallet, paid a visit,
hired himself a kilt
and highered himself
      (a helicopter)
the better to learn the lay of the land.

All week he hummed, nodded, pored over
the spectacle of Scotland's living atlas,
hovering intense as a wee professor.
Returned babbling, still high:

'Mairead (my friend) you are born richer
than I. Just think! The moonscabbed rocks,
the chiselled sweep of mossy coasts
– raw ancientness still-defined,
nested in machairs of windraked sand
in gullies of green shrubbery and secrets
in the vivid swells and tumbling slopes
– all of this I adored
      until then
      Lewis
a humble brinescrubbed stone, sparse, uncomplex,
itself enshrined in
itself, the tiny jewelled stone
of Scotland's immense zen garden.'

Elegy

Last night I dreamt of seals
immersed in a swampy grey sea

as nubs of invisible salt
buried and more buried in colourless flesh.

Before I woke, you had become less real
than this: my eyes drifting between

your new red coat, your blue gloves
and your grey brush on the window sill

still quivering with a few white hairs.